OUR GOD LIVES!

A collection of inspirational meditations

Faye Roots

ISBN: Softcover   978-1-5035-0938-2
        Hardcover   978-1-5035-0939-9
        EBook   978-1-5035-0937-5

Print information available on the last page

Rev. date: 08/25/2015

To order additional copies of this book, contact:
Xlibris
1-888-795-4274
www.Xlibris.com
Orders@Xlibris.com

The Meditation Book Prayer

Heavenly Father,

I pray for each person who reads this book. I ask that as they journey, they, in their turn may be prompted to offer up a prayer for the people or the incidents recorded. In this way together we may impart a blessing to folks in Nursing Homes, ones who grieve, or to simply share spiritually in the lives of others. May God's Blessings and Peace abound to you. In Jesus' Name a-men

Faye Roots

BECAUSE I AM

'I am the Alpha and the Omega, the Beginning and the End' says the Lord. 'Who is and Who was and Who is to come the Almighty.' Rev.1:8 N.K.J.

We sat by the river in canvas chairs, my elderly father-in-law, my husband and I. In the water in front of us three fishermen stood patiently fishing. In one hour we saw an amazing diversity of human life and nature. Deep within I felt a call to prayer.

In quick succession the first two fisherman each caught a fish. Both were small but of two different species. One was a bream – the other a whiting. They were returned to the river and we watched them swim away. The third fisherman caught a seagull.

The bird dived onto his bait and got its wing hooked and tangled in the line. A rescue team – three children, and his wife with a knife, swam out to help. After a lot of struggle and distress the bird flew away. It looked back at us from a ship's mast in mid-stream.

A couple walked by with a border collie dog and a very young puppy. Cycling elderly people, jogging young people, folks with infants in prams, all passed before our eyes. Some were smiling and friendly. Others appeared distracted, angry and even sad. We heard words of beauty and encouragement uttered but angry and impatient words also pierced the atmosphere. The hour began with brilliant sunshine and ended with a rush to cars as the wind chilled and a storm threatened.

Paul wrote of Christ to the Colossians. Col 1 (16a,17) *For by Him all things were created. All things were created through Him and for Him. He is before all things and in Him all things consist. N.K.J.*

MEDITATIVE THOUGHT

The universe is vast. Humanity diverse. Divine Love holds it all together

Revelation: 22:14 Blessed are those who do His commandments that they may have
the right to the Tree of Life and may enter through the gates into the city

A CHILD'S LEGACY

For the Lamb who is in the midst of the throne will shepherd them and lead them to living fountains of water. And God will wipe away every tear from their eyes. Rev.7:17 N.K.J.

The classes of Grade Two and Three children sat in fascinated silence as Bronson shared his dreams.

'I saw a playground of children and everything was bright and under a huge light. There was someone there but I couldn't see who it was. There was a lot of love and I wasn't worried or frightened. I also saw a golden fountain – it was beautiful. The water kept flowing. It just never ran out – lots and lots of water. It never ran dry.'

For two years the small boy had battled leukaemia. His classmates had journeyed with him. Along the way they had loved and encouraged him. They painted lots of pictures and played, sang, laughed and cried together. But it was in the final weeks of his life in the sharing of his dreams that he sowed a rich legacy to the whole school community. He was only eight when he died yet no one who knew him will ever forget his courage – the radiance of his smile, or the things he shared that made even the most cynical seek for meaning in their lives.

Today there is an auditorium and a nature walk to commemorate Bronson's life. Children can walk or sit in the quietness. The image of the golden fountain of lasting water somehow lingers in the memories of us all.

MEDITATION THOUGHT

The illness and death of a child changes the lives of everyone around them

A child's Vision of a golden fountain

ABANDONED

The Lord watches over the stranger, He relieves the fatherless and the widow

Psalm 146v9 (NKJ)

'What can I do? My father left us at the beginning of the year. We have not seen or heard from him since. Life suxs!!'

She is only eleven and her letter touched a deep chord within me. My own father was not absent but distant. Wartime experiences and his own troubled childhood made him a good provider. But, he was often withdrawn in contact with his children. Love was never the issue - we somehow always knew he loved us. This did not stop me from asking the same question "what can I do?"

Talking and sharing with Mandy seemed to help her. There was nothing she could do except firstly deal with life around her. She began to shower love on her mother and the little ones. Then, when the time was right, we spoke together about God's Love. The Father's Love that never fails.

I don't know what the future holds for this child. I only know that listening to her helped. Gentle direction helped. God focus helped. I believe HE is moving in her life. She is less stressed. She now prays for her family and her dad. She tells me she 'feels' she is doing something.

MEDITATIVE THOUGHT

Our life experiences – the pains and the joys - can bring comfort and hope to others.

Even an image of abandonment evokes feelings of loneliness and loss

BEAUTIFUL SYMPHONY

Imitate me, just as I also imitate Christ – 1 Cor 11:1

I was walking with the dogs down a quiet forest road. High in the treetops a bird sang. Its drawn-out, infinitely sweet whistled call was haunting and beautiful. It had a longing, lonely, penetrating appeal. I wanted to answer. I tried to imitate but my whistle was imperfect. It was but a thin echo of the original.

Somewhere far away another bird began to sing – then another and another.

The trees rang with a symphony of glorious music. The dogs sat with their ears pricked. They were transfixed by the sound. It became a chorus so beautiful that the first haunting cry was absorbed into the unity of collective refrain.

Jesus said: *"A new commandment I give to you that you love one another as I have loved you"* John 13:34(a).NKJ.

If we are to imitate Christ then perhaps our love expressed in smiles, kindness and gentleness – in response to anger and abuse – or, forgiveness and peace in the midst of conflict and disharmony, may be shaky and imperfect but in God's Purposes it too could be the beginning of far-reaching and transforming symphonies of blessing.

MEDITATIVE THOUGHT

Imitating Christ may not be perfectly done but can have powerful impact.

A special Prayer for: ALL WALKING LIFE ALONE WITHOUT CHRIST

BLACKOUT

Jesus said: I am the light of the world. Whoever follows me will never walk in darkness but will have the light of life. John 8:12 N.K.J.

For several days, our house was lashed by high winds and frequent, heavy rain showers. After years of drought it was reason for thanksgiving but one late afternoon the power suddenly failed. In the chilly darkness the violent outside sounds suddenly seemed louder more terrifying and threatening.

We had torches but lit instead one large candle and placed it on a table in the centre of the room.

This one light transformed the whole house. We felt warmer, comforted and the darkness was pushed back from the circle of light.

The words of Jesus, that He is the perpetual Light in the darkness , is a wonderful and powerful promise. When, by faith, He is made the centre of our lives the potential is there for His transforming Grace to work in ALL our circumstances. The sorrow or disappointments may not be removed but His Presence holds our spirits firm and enables Him to work something good even in our darkest times. (Romans 8:28).

MEDITATIVE THOUGHT

Can we bless someone by sharing His light in this day?

Special Prayer for:

Folks living in darkness without HOPE

BROKEN CONNECTIONS

Rejoice in hope, patient in tribulations – continuing steadfast in prayer. Romans 12:12 NKJ

I turned on the tap. Nothing happened. No water came out! I ran to check the pump

in the shed. Yes, it was still working. A pipe had broken. Water in gushing bursts had drowned the shed floor and was flowing away, wasting a valuable resource. I disconnected the power and beneath the now muddy back lawn, was finally able to turn off the water supply from the draining large water storage tank.

It is important in our relationship with God that we are securely 'connected'. To maintain healthy spiritual lives, we need to be constantly connected through Christ in prayer then maintained and nurtured by the Word and His Spirit.

If one link is broken the precious flow of God in our lives – our ability to care, love, and be strong in faith, can be drained away by the eroding circumstances of daily life.

MEDITATIVE THOUGHT

A relationship with God must be nurtured and maintained

A broken God connection can drain our lives of Peace and Hope

CALLED OUT OF THE BOAT

God has chosen the foolish things of the world to put to shame the wise, and God has chosen the weak things of the world to put to shame the things which are mighty.

1 Corinthians 1v27

During the time of great heartache in my home state when an historic flood washed away infrastructure and lives I was in absolute despair. What could I do? I was too old to physically repair damage and just praying seemed insufficient. I knew many people were organising aid parcels, making things for flood victims and generally 'doing' their bit to help. When I believed I had actually heard what God was calling me to do I was filled with questions. 'That is so simple. That is foolish.'

Loving, standing beside people and encouraging them. Giving them a little gift of a butterfly a symbol of 'Divine Love, Hope and New Life.' It all seemed the epitome of foolishness. But, God had gone before me and I witnessed many miracles of healing comfort.

Good ideas often come to nothing. When God is behind the inspiration the results are profound. His Love, Grace and Hope will always transform lives.

Peter followed Jesus onto the water (Matthew 14:29) but only after the Lord had told him to 'Come'. As we too learn to wait on the Lord He will lead and guide us.

MEDITATIVE THOUGHT

Sometimes God is not in the boat and He calls us to follow Him in trust and faith onto waters of uncertainty.

Following our Lord can often seem foolish in the eyes of the world

CONTAGIOUS LOVE

Zacchaeus stood there and said to the Lord, "Look half of my possessions I will give to the poor and if I have defrauded anyone of anything I will pay back four times as much."

Luke 19 v8 (NRSV)

After days of rain, sunshine flooded the room. It was a welcome blessing.

I sat at the head of a table. There were six young people gathered around. It was a Christian Spiritual Discussion Group.

The theme for the day was **Changed by the Love of Jesus**. We were reading the Gospel of Luke and discussing the changed lives of Zacchaeus, Mary, Martha, and Peter. We also discussed how the rich young man chose his money as his main life focus.

I told them lives are being changed even today by Christ's Love.

One of the girls made the comment, 'Those who followed Jesus continued to find His Love. Would that Love in them then be shared with others?' I nodded in agreement.

I was impacted then by how powerful a truth this is.

It is only as we 'connect' with Jesus today in prayer, bible reading, meditations, journalling etc that we can follow the Beloved. Then, it is HIS LOVE in us that becomes as Christ to a needing world.

It really is this life-changing LOVE that should be our main ministry.

The beautiful day of brilliant sunshine suddenly seemed just like the transformation of a life 'changed by the Love of Jesus'.

MEDITATIVE THOUGHT

Being as Christ in the world is as important as Doing for Him in the world.

Divine Love blazes like a new day – His Love through us can change lives

DANCING HOPE

'My Grace is sufficient for you for my power is made perfect in weakness.'

2 Cor 12:9 (NIV)

She is paralysed from below her waist and has been wheelchair-bound since the age of four. The Convention choir was singing:

> *'We will dance on the streets that are golden, the glorious Bride and the great Son of Man'. The song expressed from Revelations 21 the promise of Christ's return and the New Jerusalem with streets of gold. Then, every tear will be dried and all brokenness restored.*

I reached out and took her hand. Together we worshipped the One who gives hope, beauty and purpose to all our lives.

Kate is a teacher and her Christian faith continues to witness and inspire children and parents. Hundreds have been touched by her life as she humbly goes about her normal sphere of living.

MEDITATIVE THOUGHT

Christ gives LIFE meaning in all circumstances

Dancing Hope reflected in the beauty and innocence of Childhood

TRANSFORMED DESPAIR

Read: Ephesians 3: 14-21

To know the love of Christ which passes knowledge that you may be filled with all the fullness of God v:19 (N.K.J.)

The boy locked himself in the school tuckshop and screamed he would talk to no one but his RE (scripture) teacher – me. He would not come out and when the class teacher phoned I drove to the school. I asked for permission to embrace the child if needed and was given freedom to pray and minister however necessary.

He opened the door and ran straight into my arms. 'Pray for me,' he

sobbed. 'My Granddad is dying and no one else in this world loves me like he does. Everyone else thinks I'm 'a waste of space'. He cried out the story of his grandfather's cancer and his estranged and broken relationships with separated parents.

We prayed together that he would know the love of Jesus and the Presence of God to help him through the sorrow.

God answered the prayer. He told later of warmth and comfort which enveloped him. A calm, transformed boy returned to his lessons a short time after.

Carl is now a High School leader and testifies that one day he discovered God truly loved him.

MEDITATIVE THOUGHT

A hug and God-time can strengthen and help restore broken hearts and lives

New pathways open up when lives are transformed by Divine Love

DISCIPLINE IN LITTLE THINGS

In luke15:8,9,10 Jesus tells a Parable of a lost Coin.

He also said in Luke 19v17 : Because you were faithful in a very little, have authority over ten cities.

Three important identification cards were missing from my husband's wallet. Had they been stolen? Were they lost? We made a check of all likely places then for security he cancelled the Visa Card.

We had planned a day out so while he walked the dogs, I began a quick clean up and swept the floors. I prayed as I worked that if the cards were in the house I would find them. Hurriedly, I swept the simulated timber floors but planned a quick 'main areas' only. *'Be faithful in the little things'* – I sensed a God prompting.

Reluctantly, I decided to sweep properly. I found the cards behind the computer leads near the wall of the office. Earlier, when Dave had turned on the computer, as he reached over, they must have fallen from his open wallet.

This small incident reminded me clearly that it is often in the 'little' necessities of our Christian Life that discipline to complete our responsibilities can prepare us for bigger challenges.

MEDITATION THOUGHT

What 'little' thing could I do this day to make the life of someone else better?

A lost object when found does not increase in material value but soars in appreciative value

RESTORATION

As you have received Christ Jesus the Lord so walk in Him rooted and built up in Him and established in the faith.

Col. 2:6,7a (N.K.J.)

The cutting down of the tree was a necessity. Its powerful trunk with extending branches and extremely dry leaf structure was considered a fire hazard to our home.

It made me sad to see a once proud tree, reduced to a stark, dead, metre high trunk, ring-barked at ground level waiting for the final chain saw cut.

Then we had a few days of rain. Today from beneath the ground (below the damaged trunk) green shoots are pushing skywards. This new tree will be different from the original. It certainly will not be tall and stately. Even the verdant green leaves are softer and smaller. They do however surge with life from the nutrients in the root system below.

I believe that for all whose lives are rooted in God He is able, despite circumstances that might even seem to destroy us, to still make something beautiful out of what remains.

MEDITATIVE THOUGHT

From out of what may look like death and destruction to us - God still brings forth abundant life.

BEAUTY RISES WHEN LIFE IS RENEWED

IMPORTANCE OF FOCUS

Whatever things are of good report, if there is any virtue and if there is anything praiseworthy – meditate on these things. Phil 4: 8b N.K.J.

I was reminded of Paul's closing instructions to the church at Philippi last month. I was at an awards night for creative fiction short story writers. The winning story was read aloud. It was a brilliant piece of writing. The story was about a teenage suicide. It was graphic. The ending gave no message of hope. We were all upset. Some people were crying.

This dark depression in the room was lifted by a sudden excited cry from a child outside in the foyer.

'Mum, Mum come and see!' he called. 'It's a full moon. It's like a beautiful golden ball.' His youthful laughter and joy brought back smiles to downcast faces.

With Christ's Presence within (Col 1:27) we should be educated and informed people. We need to be prayers and helpers. Our greatest calling however, is to be hope sowers. We can only do this effectively if we keep our focus on Christ and balance our lives in the truths of tragedy with certainty of God's Grace, Love, Forgiveness, and Hope in Christ.

MEDITATIVE THOUGHT

Can I share something beautiful, holy and of good news with someone today?

A SPECIAL PRAYER FOR CREATIVE, GIFTED PEOPLE

WHO DO NOT KNOW GOD's REDEMPTIVE LOVE.

FREEDOM TO SOAR

Jesus said: 'If the Son makes you free you shall be free indeed' John 8.36

I heard the bird cry and knew with heart-stopping certainty our kitten had caught it. (We intended to put a bell round the neck of this new arrival but because she was very young had underestimated her hunting abilities).

I could see the beautiful blue plumage of the small bird as the kitten squeezed behind the lounge chair proudly holding her catch.

The bird cried out again and I lunged behind the chair instinctively pinching the only part of the kitten I could reach – her back foot.

Surprised, she opened her mouth and the bird escaped.

With lightning speed and franticly flapping wings, it flew around the room and out the open door. Screeching, it flew to the top of one of the largest trees. We live in a bush area so there are many trees.

The whole tree suddenly erupted with sound. It started with a deep throated chirp of welcome and grew and grew until hundreds of invisible birds joined in. Then, from high in the air came the raucous caws of flying crows, and in the distance the kookaburras laughed their territorial laughs. The rooster in the fowl house crowed. The dog ran round and round the house barking.

The sounds together made a chorus of exultant joy.

What a wonderful harmony of joyous sound there must be in heaven over every sinner who repents. (Luke 15 v10)

This incident with the bird caused me to rejoice again in the beauty and wonder of what Jesus Christ has done for me. Undeserved forgiveness through His sacrificial death. I am free to soar to God in my spirit. I am able to come before my Father in heaven as His child and **know** I am loved.

Praise God -in Christ- I too am truly free

STRENGTH IN HIS PRESENCE

A great prophet has risen among us and "God has visited His People:

Luke 7: 16b (NKJ)

God has visited His people

My frail elderly cousin inspired all who knew her. In the armchair in her Nursing Home room she would sit for her 'God Time'. Peaceful and still she remained for the hour she requested of the Staff to be *left alone*.

'It's all about the Spirit' she told me. Pentecost changed everything. Jesus really is **with** me. Her daily worship, in absolute stillness, gave her His Strength to live an abundant life until she journeyed home to Him in 2012.

The old Testament Prophet Elijah appealed to God and received His Power to heal a widow's son (1 KINGS 17: 21-24)

Jesus healed a widow's son in His own Authority. (Luke 7:11-16) No wonder the onlookers were shocked – Jesus the Prophet – God has visited His People.

We can rejoice that **now** because of the coming of the Spirit - Christ's Presence with us is more than a visit – it is a permanent reality.

MEDITATIVE THOOUGHT

God The Holy Spirit – Sanctifier – gentle as a dove, powerful as a roaring fire.

Printed in the United States
By Bookmasters